LEVEL B
Comprehension PLUS

Dr. Diane Lapp
Dr. James Flood

Modern Curriculum Press

All photos ©Pearson Learning unless otherwise noted.

Photographs

5: Bill Beatty/Animals Animals. 6: Gloria Schlaepfer. 8: Joe McDonald/Bruce Coleman, Inc. 25: *l.* Kennan Ward/The Stock Market; *r.* ©Stephen Dalton/The National Audubon Society Collection/Photo Researchers, Inc. 26: Duncan Smith/PhotoDisc, Inc. 33: Denis Scott/The Stock Market. 34: Ken Graham/Stone. 37, 41 *l.*, 45: SuperStock, Inc. 38, 122 *t.*: Hans Reinhard/Bruce Coleman, Inc. 41: *r.* D. Fleetham/OSF/Animals Animals. 46: ARS, NY Private Collection/Art Resource, NY. 53: The Seeing Eye, Inc. 54: Courtesy of San Francisco SPCA Hearing Dog Program. 56: Corbis. 57: Mindstorm Communications. 58: NASA/Science Photo Library/Photo Researchers, Inc. 98: *t.* John M. Roberts/The Stock Market; *m.t.* Philip H. Coblentz/Stone; *m.m.* John Gerlach/Earth Scenes; *m.b.* George D. Dodge/Bruce Coleman, Inc. 98 *b.*, 100: Don Brown/Earth Scenes. 121: Michael Fogden/Bruce Coleman, Inc. 122: *m.t.* W. Gregory Brown, *m.b.* Miriam Agron, *b.* Steve Earley/Animals Animals.

Illustrations

9, 69, 70: Laurie Struck Long. 13, 14, 101, 102, 104: Meredith Johnson. 21, 22: Joy Allen. 29, 30, 31: David Wenzel. 44, 81, 82, 84: Teri Weidner. 52: Amy Wummer. 62, 113, 116: Michael Reid. 65, 66, 68, 97: Anne Kennedy. 73, 74, 85, 86: Molly Delaney. 77, 78: Jeff LeVan. 106: Jackie Urbanovic. 109, 110, 112: Elizabeth Allen. 118: Will Hamilton.

Cover art: photo montage: Wendy Wax. background: Doug Bowles.

Design development: MKR Design, New York: Manuela Paul, Deirdre Newman, Marta K. Ruliffson.

Design: Lisa Ann Arcuri.

ISBN: 0-7652-2181-0
Printed in the United States of America

20 21 22 23 24 25   V003   15 14 13 12 11 10

Modern Curriculum Press
Pearson Learning Group

1-800-321-3106
www.pearsonlearning.com

Table of Contents

Comprehending Text

Story Structure

Word Study

Document Reading

Making Judgments

When you decide what you think about a story or an article, you are **making a judgment.** To make a judgment, think about whether you agree or disagree with what you are reading.

Read the letters. Decide what you think about how to make friends.

Dear Aunt Beth,

We are moving and I am worried about my new school. I want to make friends there. Do you know how I can do it? Help!

Love, Shannon

Dear Shannon,

Making friends is easy. Be friendly to the other children. Say hello and tell them your name. Don't forget to smile, too. Take turns when you play with others. Soon you will have many new friends!

Love, Aunt Beth

Tip

When you read a story, decide what you think about the characters and what they do. When you read an article, decide what you think about the things the author is telling about.

Draw a line under all the sentences that you think are good ideas for making new friends.

Say hello.   Play fairly.   Take turns.

Don't talk.   Smile.   Sit by yourself.

Read the story about helping friends. Think about what the characters do. Decide if you agree or disagree.

A Helping Hand

Rosie liked helping her friends. "Friends help each other," she always said.

Sometimes Rosie's help wasn't very helpful, though. She was a little careless.

When she used her garden hose to water her neighbor's plants, Rosie watered the chairs, too. When Mr. and Mrs. West sat down in their backyard chairs, they were very surprised.

Rosie's face turned red. "Uh-oh, " she said. "I'm sorry. I was just trying to help."

When Rosie tried to help her friend Tammy carry things home from school, she dropped Tammy's painting. It fell in a puddle.

"Oh, no!" thought Rosie. "I was only trying to help again. Now I feel bad."

Rosie thought about a way she could change.

"I know," said Rosie. "I will ask people if they need my help first."

Now Rosie always asks before she helps. She also remembers to be careful.

Checking Comprehension

Write the answer to each question on the lines.

1. Why did Rosie think she needed to change?

_____

_____

2. What did Rosie learn about helping friends?

_____

Practicing Comprehension Skills

Read the questions. Write the answers on the lines.

3. Do you think Rosie will try to water Mr. and Mrs. West's plants again? Why or why not?

_____

_____

4. Rosie always said, "I'm sorry." Do you think that was a good thing to say? Why or why not?

_____

_____

5. Why do you think it is good to ask people before you help them?

_____

_____

6. Why do you think Rosie decided to think about how she helped people? Fill in the circle.

○ She was mad at her friend Tammy.

○ She wanted to be careless.

○ She felt bad when she made mistakes.

Practicing Vocabulary

Read what Rosie wrote in her journal.
Write a word from the box to finish each sentence.

watered	helpful	surprise	puddle	careless

7. Today I was _____ and made some

mistakes. I wanted to _____ my

neighbors. They did not like it when I

_____ their chairs. I wasn't very

_____ to my friend Tammy when I

dropped her painting in a _____. I will

be more careful, and I will ask before I help people.

Writing a Journal Entry
On another sheet of paper, write a journal entry.
Draw a picture of a friend. Write sentences telling
why you think you will stay friends.

Point of View

When you read, think about who is telling the story. Sometimes a character tells the story. The character uses the words **I**, **me**, and **we**. Sometimes a speaker who is not a character tells the story. The speaker uses the words **he**, **she**, **it**, and **they**.

Read each story. Think about who is telling the story.

Story 1	Story 2
I like being a strawberry farmer. Each morning I pick the ripest strawberries. Then I am ready for the big outdoor market.	Mr. Lopez likes being a strawberry farmer. Each morning he picks the ripest strawberries. Then he is ready for the big outdoor market.

Who is telling Story 1? Fill in the circle.

○ a speaker who is not a character

○ the farmer

○ the farmer's wife

Who is telling Story 2? Fill in the circle.

○ a speaker who is not a character

○ the farmer

○ the farmer's wife

Tip

The clue words **I**, **me**, and **we** or **he**, **she**, and **it** will help you know who is telling the story.

Read each story about Frank the rooster. Think about who is telling each story.

The Rooster Who Forgot to Crow

The Day I Forgot to Crow

"Cock-a-doodle-doo!" crowed Frank the rooster.

Farmer Elaine woke up and milked the cows. The chickens laid eggs. The horses pulled the wagon. Everyone was busy except Frank.

Frank felt useless, so he decided to help. He worked all day. By dark he was exhausted. The next morning Frank was asleep when the sun rose. A sleeping rooster doesn't crow.

"I hope you had a good reason for not waking me today," Farmer Elaine told Frank later. "Now I can't get all my work done."

Frank finally saw how important his job was. "Cock-a-doodle-doo!" he crowed proudly.

"Cock-a-doodle-doo!" I crowed loudly from the roof of the barn.

Farmer Elaine woke up and milked the cows. The chickens laid eggs. The horses pulled the wagon. Everyone was busy except me.

I felt useless, so I decided to help. I worked all day. By dark I was exhausted. The next morning I was asleep when the sun came up. Because I was sleeping, I did not crow.

"I hope you had a good reason for not waking me today," Farmer Elaine said to me later. "Now I can't get all my work done."

I finally saw how important my job was. "Cock-a-doodle-doo!" I crowed proudly.

Checking Comprehension

Write the answers to the questions on the lines.

1. Why do you think a rooster is important on a farm?

   _____

2. Why do you think is it important for everyone
   on a farm or in a family to have their own jobs?

   _____

   _____

Practicing Comprehension Skills

Read each question. Fill in the circle next to the answer.

3. Who is telling "The Rooster Who Forgot to Crow"?
   ○ Frank the rooster   ○ Farmer Elaine
   ○ a speaker who is not a character

4. What words show you who is telling the story?
   ○ you, your   ○ he, his   ○ I, my, we

5. Who is telling "The Day I Forgot to Crow"?
   ○ Frank the rooster   ○ a horse
   ○ a speaker who is not a character

6. What words show you who is telling the story?
   ○ you, your   ○ he, she   ○ I, my, me

Rewrite the sentences so that Frank is telling the story.

7. The next morning Frank woke up.
"Cock-a-doodle-doo!" he crowed.

_____

8. Frank agreed to do only his job from now on.

_____

Practicing Vocabulary

Write words from the box to finish the poem.

reason	crow	decided	asleep	useless

9. Frank _____ to sleep late in his shed.

It was _____ to pull him out of his bed.

"I was _____, you know.

I was too tired to _____!"

Was the _____ the poor rooster said.

Writing a Story
Think about a farm animal. Use another sheet of paper to write a story that tells what the animal does each day. Let the animal tell the story.

Character

The people or animals in stories are the **characters.** Read what the author says about a character. You can learn what characters look like, what they think, how they feel, and what they say and do.

Read about Fox and Owl. Think about the characters.

Fox liked to cook fancy meals. Today he wished he had a friend to eat with.

Just then, Owl flew by and said, "Something smells good! May I eat with you?"

"Yes!" said Fox. "I made cricket and berry stew."

"Mmmm," said Owl. "Tomorrow I'll cook you my favorite food."

Fill in the circles to answer the questions.

Who are the characters in the story?

◯ Fox   ◯ Cricket   ◯ Owl

What does the author tell you about Fox?

◯ Fox has a spider friend.   ◯ Fox cooks fancy meals.

What does the author tell you about Owl?

◯ Owl is mean.   ◯ Owl likes to cook, too.

Tip

As you read a story, look for clues that tell what the characters are like. This will help you understand and enjoy the story.

STRATEGY: Literary Elements: Character   **69**

On Your Own

Read the story. Look for words that tell what Lani thinks and how she feels.

Lani Speaks Up

Lani walked down the hall of her new school. Mr. Reed, her new teacher, met her at the classroom door. He greeted Lani with a big smile and a big hearty voice.

"Hi, Lani," Mr. Reed boomed out. "We've been waiting for you. Class, our new student has arrived. Let's welcome Lani to our classroom with a great big hello."

"Hello!" everyone said.

"Hello," Lani said very quietly. Her voice was almost a whisper. Lani was very shy. She wondered if anyone would like her here. She was worried about making new friends.

Lani found her desk and sat down quickly. Behind her she heard a girl giggling. Lani wondered if the girl was laughing at her. She felt even more shy than usual. Lani did not say anything all morning.

At lunchtime, the girl behind Lani tapped her on the shoulder. She said, "My name is Lani, too. Isn't that funny?"

Lani looked at the girl and smiled. Then she spoke up. "Two girls named Lani in one class! That's amazing," she said. All of a sudden she didn't feel shy anymore.

That day, Lani and Lani ate lunch together. Both girls talked and talked.

Checking Comprehension

Write the answer to each question on the lines.

1. What would you have done to make Lani feel more comfortable about being in a new school?

   _____

   _____

2. How did Lani change from the beginning of the story to the end?

   _____

   _____

Practicing Comprehension Skills

Read each question. Fill in the circle next to the answer.

3. How did Lani speak at first?

   ○ very quietly   ○ very loudly   ○ very angrily

4. Which word does the author use to describe Lani?

   ○ silly   ○ mad   ○ shy

5. What happens when Lani meets the other Lani?

   ○ She cries.   ○ She yells.   ○ She speaks up.

6. Write words on each line to tell about Lani.

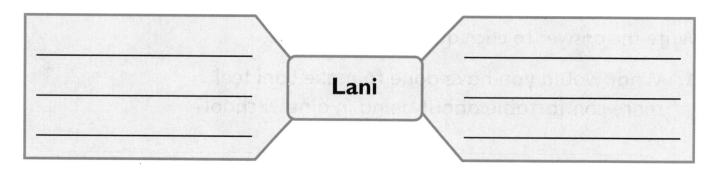

Lani

Practicing Vocabulary

Write the word from the box that matches each meaning.

whisper	giggling	hearty	arrived	smile

_____ **7.** laughing

_____ **8.** came to

_____ **9.** big, loud

_____ **10.** soft, low way of speaking

_____ **11.** grin

Writing About a Character
On another sheet of paper, draw a picture of a story character doing something. Write sentences to tell about your character.

Plot

The **plot** of a story is made up of the most important parts. The plot is what happens at the beginning, middle, and end of the story.

Read the story about Mickey. Think about the most important things that happen.

Mickey was smiling in his sleep. He was dreaming about the big baseball game today. It was time for Mickey to wake up. He needed to be at the field early. He had forgotten to set his alarm, though. Then Mickey's dog Mugs saved the day. He jumped on Mickey's bed and barked. Mickey woke up. "Thank you, Mugs!" he said. He made it to the baseball field right on time.

Draw a line under the most important things that happened in this story.

It was the day of the big game.

Mickey was smiling.

Mugs woke Mickey.

Mickey was on time after all.

Mickey was dreaming.

Tip

To understand what a story is about, think about the most important things that happen at the beginning, the middle, and the end.

Read the story about Lucy's favorite pet. Think about what happens at the beginning, middle, and end of the story.

Lucy's Surprise

by Reeve Lindbergh

Lucy had lots of chickens. The one she loved best was a little brown hen named Henrietta. Henrietta liked to peck at Lucy's shoelaces.

"Don't eat my sneakers!" Lucy would say. Henrietta would tilt her head to one side, almost as if she were listening. It always made Lucy laugh.

One morning when Lucy came to feed the chickens, Henrietta was missing. Lucy looked everywhere. Where was Henrietta? The little hen wasn't there the next day, or the next, or the one after that. Lucy was very sad. She told the other chickens, "You are just chickens. I miss my friend Henrietta."

Then one day, Henrietta returned! Six baby chicks ran behind her. Two of the chicks pulled at Lucy's shoelaces.

"Hey! Don't eat my sneakers!" Lucy said.

Henrietta's chicks all put their heads to the side. It was almost as if they were listening, too! Lucy laughed.

Checking Comprehension

Write the answer to each question on the line.

1. Why did Henrietta leave?

   _____

2. Why was Lucy so happy when Henrietta came back?

   _____

Practicing Comprehension Skills

Write words to finish each sentence in the story map.

Beginning

3. Lucy's favorite hen is _____.
4. Henrietta liked to _____.

Middle

5. One morning, Henrietta _____.
6. Lucy looked everywhere. She felt _____.

End

7. Henrietta returned with _____.
8. Two baby chicks _____.

Fill in each blank with the words **beginning, middle,** or **end.**

9. At the _____ of the story,
Henrietta returns with six chicks.

10. At the _____ of the story,
Lucy's favorite hen is Henrietta.

11. In the _____ of the story,
Henrietta is missing.

Practicing Vocabulary

Write the word from the box that matches the underlined
word or words.

laughed	returned	Don't	wasn't	shoelaces

_____ 12. Henrietta <u>was not</u> with the other hens.

_____ 13. Henrietta <u>came back</u> with six chicks.

_____ 14. Lucy <u>giggled</u> when she saw the chicks.

_____ 15. The <u>ties</u> on Lucy's sneakers were red.

_____ 16. Lucy said, "<u>Do not</u> eat my sneakers!"

Writing a Story
On another sheet of paper, write a short story
about a surprise you had. Remember to tell what
happens in the beginning, the middle, and the end.

LESSON 19

Setting

When and where a story happens is called the **setting.** The setting can be a real place or a make-believe place. The setting can be long ago, or even in the future. As you read, think about the time and place in the story.

Read the story. Think about where and when the story happens.

Yoshi looked out the window at the clouds. His parents were asleep in the seats next to him. They had been flying all night.

It was seven o'clock in the morning. Suddenly, the clouds were gone. Yoshi could see the ground below.

Yoshi woke his parents. "I can see buildings! There is a baseball stadium."

Then the pilot said, "Welcome to the United States."

Fill in the circle next to the correct answer.

Where does the story happen?

○ on a bus   ○ in a car   ○ in an airplane

When does the story happen?

○ morning   ○ afternoon   ○ night

Tip

When you read a story, the pictures can give clues about the setting. A title can, too. The setting of a story is where and when the story happens.

Read the letter. Look for clues that tell the setting.

Home, Sweet Home

Dear Luis,

Here I am in our new house. It took us four days to drive here. We arrived two days ago, just in time for the 4th of July. Things are really different here. There isn't a lot of rain, so there's no grass. We have little red rocks in our yard instead! There aren't a lot of trees, either. Instead, there are scrubby cactus plants everywhere!

The sky here is the usual blue, but it seems bigger somehow.

Mom said we wouldn't need to wear heavy clothes much in the desert. She was right. It's 105 degrees today! We have funny little lizards running around outside our house. They like the heat. The lizards seem friendly, but I haven't been able to catch one yet.

How's my old baseball team doing? I'm going to play baseball here, too. We play at night when it's cool.

I miss you. I hope you can come for a visit this winter. We won't be able to make any snowballs, but we might be able to go swimming!

Your friend,
Josh

Checking Comprehension

Write the answer to each question on the lines.

1. How do you think Josh feels about his new home?

_____

_____

2. How are things different in the new place where
Josh lives?

_____

_____

Practicing Comprehension Skills

Fill in the circle next to the correct answer.

3. Where Josh lives now, it is _____.

○ very cold   ○ very hot   ○ always raining

4. Instead of many trees, _____ grow all around.

○ tall flowers   ○ rocks   ○ cactus plants

5. Since it's so hot, Josh will play baseball at _____.

○ night   ○ noon   ○ midnight

6. Where does Josh live now?

○ in the city   ○ in the mountains ○ in the desert

Read each sentence. Write **T** if the sentence tells something true about the story setting. Write **F** if the sentence tells something false.

_____ 7. Josh has moved far away from Luis.

_____ 8. There are whales and seagulls where Josh lives now.

_____ 9. There isn't a lot of rain where Josh lives now.

_____ 10. Cactus plants grow where Josh lives now.

_____ 11. Where Josh lives now, they play baseball at noon.

Practicing Vocabulary

Write words from the box to finish the riddle and its answer.

blue	degrees	desert	July	scrubby

12. **Riddle:** This is a place that has _____

    plants called cactus. The skies are clear and

    _____. It can get as hot as 105

    _____ in the month of _____.

    Answer: This place is the _____.

Description of a Place

On another sheet of paper, write about your favorite place. It could be a room in your home or a place you like to visit. Use words that tell your readers what the place is like.

Theme

Every story has one big idea. This big idea is the story's **theme.** As you read, think about what happens in the story and what you already know. This will help you understand the story's big idea.

Read the story and think about the big idea.

Bear sat by the river. Next to him was a big pile of fish. Then Otter strolled by.

"That sure is a lot of fish!" Otter said.

"I fished all day. Now it's time for dinner."

Suddenly, Otter got an idea. "Bear, I think I hear your mother calling. You'd better go."

"Gee, Otter, that reminds me," Bear said quickly. "I saw your father. He wants you to hurry home."

Otter raced home. Bear ate all the fish.

Draw a line under the answer.

What was Otter trying to do?

get Bear's fish   take a walk

How did Otter try to do it?

by racing Bear   by tricking Bear

What is the big idea of the story?

Don't believe everything someone tells you.

Otters are easily tricked.

Tip

Some stories have more than one big idea. To help you figure out the theme, think about the characters and what they learn in the story.

Read the story. Think about the big idea.

Raccoon and Crayfish

by Joseph Bruchac

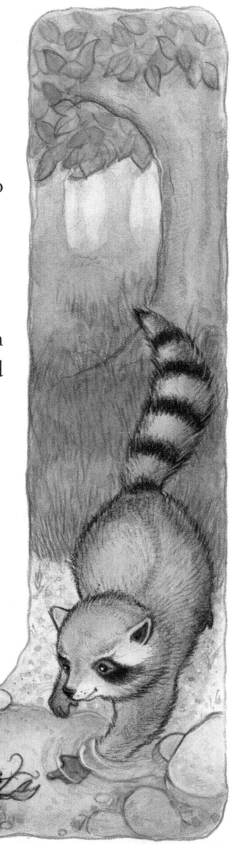

Raccoon was very hungry, so he went to the river. Crayfish was hiding under a rock. Raccoon waded into the water and reached under the rock. As soon as Raccoon touched the crayfish, it pinched him. Raccoon shook his paw and climbed out of the water.

"Crayfish," he said, "you were right to pinch me, because I wanted to eat you. I am hungry. In fact, I am starving!" Then Raccoon fell down with his eyes closed and his feet sticking up in the air.

Crayfish hurried to tell all his friends that Raccoon was dead. All the crayfish made a circle around Raccoon. They danced and sang until they were too tired to move.

Suddenly, Raccoon jumped up. "Thank you for that lovely dance," he said. Then Raccoon ate up all the foolish crayfish. As the wise ones say, "Never celebrate someone else's troubles." Remember what happened to those crayfish!

Checking Comprehension

Write the answer to each question on the lines.

1. Why did Raccoon fall down with his eyes closed and his feet sticking into the air?

   _____

2. Do you think it was smart for the crayfish to sing and dance until they were too tired to move? Tell why or why not.

   _____

   _____

Practicing Comprehension Skills

Fill in the circle before the correct answer.

3. Raccoon could be described as _____.

   ○ silly   ○ unhappy   ○ tricky

4. The crayfish could be described as _____.

   ○ foolish   ○ proud   ○ smart

5. Which would have been the smartest thing for Crayfish to do after Raccoon fell down?

   ○ hide and wait to see if Raccoon got up

   ○ have a party

   ○ play in the water

6. What is the big idea of this story?

○ Raccoons are smarter than crayfish.

○ Do not be happy about someone's troubles. You might have troubles, too.

○ Don't fish for crayfish or you might get pinched.

Practicing Vocabulary

Write a word from the box to finish each sentence.

foolish	shook	Thank	starving	waded

7.   Raccoon had not eaten and was _____.

Raccoon _____ out into the water

and grabbed a big fish. The big fish _____

its tail and splashed Raccoon.

     "It's _____ to catch me," the fish

said. "I am too big for you."

     After Raccoon ate the fish, he said, "_____

you for telling me."

Making the Reading and Writing Connection

Writing a Story
On another sheet of paper, write a story that tells a lesson. Your lesson might be about helping others or any other big idea. Ask a partner to read your story and tell what your big idea is.

Alphabetizing

LESSON 21

Look at the first letter of these words: **coach, banker, dancer.** In the alphabet, **b** comes before **c,** and **c** comes before **d.** If you put the words in **alphabetical order,** they would be **banker, coach, dancer.** Using alphabetical order can make words easier to find.

Read about one way to use alphabetical order.

This week our class learned about different workers. We all picked jobs we would like to do someday.

We drew pictures and wrote sentences to tell about each job. Then we put our pictures in a book in alphabetical order. Mine was last. Can you guess what I want to be? A zookeeper!

Write the words in alphabetical order.

| nurse | barber | farmer |

_____

| teacher | pilot | writer |

_____

Tip

To put words in alphabetical order, look at the first letter of each word. Put the words in the same order as those letters are in the alphabet.

Read the story. Think about how these children use alphabetical order.

On the Job

"I hope you'll all come and visit me soon at the gym," Kai's dad said at the end of his talk. We all clapped. Then we thanked him for coming to visit us. All week, parents had come in to talk about their jobs. They told us about what they did and where they worked. Kai's dad owned a gym in the city.

Our teacher Mrs. Cole said, "OK, class. We've learned a lot about different jobs. How can we share that information with others?"

"I know," said Amy. "We can make a mural that shows all the different places there are to work."

"I liked hearing about the factory," said George. "Which place should we show first?"

"Let's put them in alphabetical order," said Gwen.

"We can start with the computer office where Jane's mom works," said Jim. "Next we'll show the factory. Then we'll show the gym."

"I know where we can hang our mural," said Mrs. Cole. "We'll put it in the front hall of our school. This is the place where we work each day!"

Checking Comprehension

Write the answer to each question on the line.

1. Why do you think Mrs. Cole thinks the front hall is a good place to hang the mural?

   _____

2. Name some other places where people work near your home.

   _____

Practicing Comprehension Skills

Write each set of words in alphabetical order.

3.
| firehouse   airport   hotel |
| garage   bakery |

   _____

   _____

   _____

   _____

4.
| library   hospital   school |
| ranch   museum |

   _____

   _____

   _____

   _____

Put the words in alphabetical order to write a sentence.

5. pears   likes   He

   _____

Put the words in alphabetical order to write a sentence.

6. explore outer Astronauts space

_____

7. plants A trees gardener

_____

8. teeth dentist save helps A

_____

Practicing Vocabulary

Write the word from the box that belongs in each group.

| clapped | city | office | mural | gym |

9. town, village, _____

10. workplace, room, _____

11. swimming pool, skating rink, _____

12. cheered, yelled, _____

13. painting, picture, _____

Writing a Thank-You Note
Think of a worker who helps you each day at school or in your community. On a separate sheet of paper, write a thank-you note to that person.

Alphabetizing

How do you put words in **alphabetical order** when all the words start with the same letter? You use the second letter in each word.

In the name **Alex Anteater,** the second letter of the word **Alex** is **l.** The second letter of the word **Anteater** is **n.** The letter **l** comes before the letter **n** in the alphabet. The word **Alex** comes before **Anteater** in alphabetical order.

Read about the silly animal show. See if the character names are in alphabetical order.

Mrs. Doyle's class put on a silly animal show. Alex Anteater ate some gummy ants. Everyone yelled, "Yuck!" Droopy Dog did a funny trick. Sammy Seal clapped his flippers. Steve Snake crawled on the floor. He stuck out his tongue. Everyone clapped for the silly animals.

Tip

When two words start with the same letter, look at the second letter of each word to put the words in alphabetical order.

Below are names from the story. Circle YES or NO to tell if the two words are in alphabetical order.

Alex Anteater	YES	NO
Droopy Dog	YES	NO
Sammy Seal	YES	NO
Steve Snake	YES	NO

Read Julia's letter, and find out how Julia's class uses alphabetical order.

Dear Grandma and Grandpa,

I hope you are fine. I have been very busy at school. This week we wrote tongue twisters. We read them to each other. Everyone wanted to be first. Our teacher said we could read in alphabetical order. We put all of our names in order. The job was easy until we came to the letter **J.** Four kids have names that start with **J.** My name is one of them. Jay was first. Then Jessica was second. Josh came third. I was fourth, of course!

Here are my twisters. I hope you enjoy them! Don't laugh when Grandpa's tongue gets twisted.

Nina's noisy neighbors never nap.

See six silly sheep sit in soft suds.

Love,
Julia

Checking Comprehension

1. Why do you think Julia shared her tongue twisters?

   _____

   _____

2. How does Julia feel about her grandparents? How do you know?

   _____

   _____

Practicing Comprehension Skills

Write each set of words in alphabetical order.

3. noisy, neighbors, nap, Nina's

   _____

   _____

4. sheep, see, silly, suds

   _____

   _____

Write numbers to show the alphabetical order of each set of words.

5. love _____

   Julia _____

   Jessica _____

   laugh _____

6. twisters _____

   we _____

   tongue _____

   wrote _____

Write the words in alphabetical order to finish each silly tongue twister.

7. Sally, shells, selling

_____ is _____ _____.

8. butter, Betty, bread, bought, Bitter

_____ _____ _____

brown _____ and _____.

Practicing Vocabulary

Write a word from the box to finish each sentence.

enjoy	noisy	easy	Everyone	until

9. It is _____ to laugh at tongue

twisters. _____ wants to say

them. Practice _____ you can say

them well. Then _____ sharing them

with friends. Be ready for the _____

laughter!

Making the Reading and Writing Connection

Writing a Tongue Twister
Think of two names that start with the same letter.
Write the names in alphabetical order. Then use
the names to write a funny tongue twister, such as
Marsha and Mike make mushy marshmallows.

Compound Words

Sometimes words are made up of two smaller words put together. These are called **compound words.** **Football** is a compound word. It is made by putting together two smaller words, **foot** and **ball.**

As you read, look for compound words.

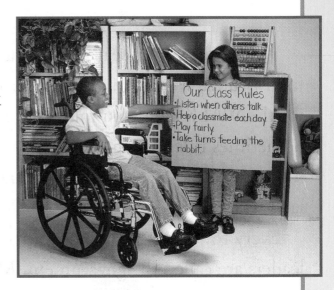

People follow rules everyday. Rules tell us what we should do. Rules help you work and play with your classmates in school.

There are special playground rules. You follow rules during a fire drill. Rules remind you to walk in the hallway and to use a crosswalk when leaving school in the afternoon. These rules keep people safe.

Write the two smaller words that make up each compound word.

_____ + _____ = everyday

_____ + _____ = playground

_____ + _____ = classmates

_____ + _____ = afternoon

_____ + _____ = hallway

_____ + _____ = crosswalk

Tip

Sometimes you can figure out the meaning of a compound word by looking at the two smaller words.

Read the article. Look for the compound words.

Meet Your Lawmakers

When you wear a seatbelt in a car, you follow rules. When you wait at a crosswalk for the WALK sign, you follow rules. Sometimes rules become laws. A law is a rule for everyone. Do you know who makes the laws where you live?

Every town has a group of leaders. These leaders are called the government. Many towns have a special leader called a mayor. This person works with other leaders in the town. These leaders help the town make its laws. People vote to elect these lawmakers.

Laws make a town a better place to live. Anyone can help make laws. Someday you may want to change something where you live. Write a letter to the mayor. The mayor listens to the people of the town. You may cause something to change for the better.

Checking Comprehension

Write the answer to each question on the lines.

1. Why do you think laws are important?

   _____

2. What can you do to help make or change laws?

   _____

Practicing Comprehension Skills

Draw a line to make a compound word. The first one is done for you.

3. fire	walk	7. play	way
4. mail	fighter	8. store	ball
5. cross	belt	9. base	ground
6. seat	box	10. run	keeper

Use a compound word you made above to finish each sentence. Write the compound word on the line.

11. Always wear a _____ when you are in a car.

12. Planes land on a _____ at the airport.

13. Put a stamp on your letter and put it in the _____.

14. A _____ told us about having a fire drill at home.

Write the compound word that means the same thing.

anyone, everyone, sometimes, lawmaker

_____ **15.** a person who makes laws

_____ **16.** every person in a group

_____ **17.** any person

_____ **18.** some of the time

Practicing Vocabulary

Write a word from the box to match each meaning.

elect	government	law	mayor	cause

19. _____ a rule people agree to obey

20. _____ leader of a community

21. _____ a group of people who make laws

22. _____ the reason for something

23. _____ choose by voting

Making the Reading and Writing Connection

Writing a Letter
Use another piece of paper to write a letter to your mayor. Suggest a new law for your community. Explain why it is a good law. Use some compound words in your letter.

Synonyms

You say, "That is a big pizza." Your friend says, "Yes, that pizza is huge." The words **big** and **huge** have almost the same meaning. Words that have the same or almost the same meaning are called **synonyms.**

Read about a very special house. Look for synonyms the writer uses to tell the story.

Would you like to live in a house on the sea? Sean does. His home is a houseboat. Sean likes his home, because he enjoys the ocean.

Sean has chores to do on the boat. When it is docked, Sean helps his dad wash the boat, and he takes out the trash. Sean knows his jobs are important.

Sean has his own tiny room on the boat. It may be small, but it's big enough for doing homework or playing games with friends when they visit.

Write a word from the story that means the same or almost the same as each word below.

Tip
To find out if two words are synonyms, use both words in the same sentence. Ask yourself, "Do both sentences have the same meaning?"

chores _____   enjoys _____

sea _____   tiny _____

house _____

Read the article about homes. Look for synonyms the writer uses.

A Home for Everyone

People live in all kinds of homes. People choose their homes for different reasons.

Cities don't have a lot of room for houses. Many people live in apartments. Each apartment building can have many stories, or floors. Each floor might have ten or more families!

Farmers need a large amount of land. Crops and farm animals need space. Farmers build their houses in the country where there is lots of open land.

Some people who live in hot deserts make clay homes. The thick clay walls keep the rooms cool.

People in very rainy places sometimes build homes on stilts. These posts lift the houses up high. No one worries about rain showers. When rain storms bring floods, the stilt houses stay dry.

People in cold places sometimes raise their homes above the ground, too. Frozen ground is ground that usually has a lot of water in it. If a house is built on frozen earth, warmth from the house could melt the frozen ground. Then the house would sink into the mud.

Look at the homes around you. See how the homes fit the place where you live.

Checking Comprehension

Write the answer to the question on the lines.

1. How do people choose the best home to live in?

   _____

2. Why are there so many different kinds of homes?

   _____

Practicing Comprehension Skills

Write a word from the box that is a synonym for each word in the web.

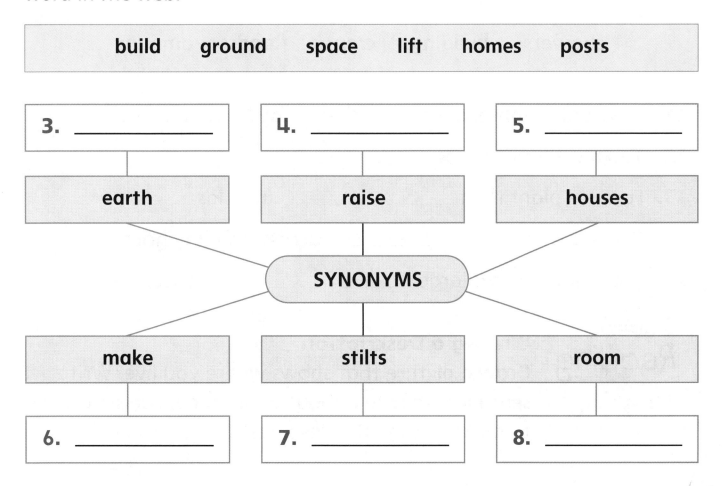

| build | ground | space | lift | homes | posts |

3. _____ earth

4. _____ raise

5. _____ houses

SYNONYMS

make 6. _____

stilts 7. _____

room 8. _____

Fill in the circle next to the word that is a synonym for the underlined word.

9. A house could <u>sink</u> into the mud.

　○ fall 　　　　　○ wash 　　　　　○ rise

10. The earth <u>below</u> is frozen.

　○ above 　　　　○ underneath 　　　○ beside

Practicing Vocabulary

Write a word from the box to finish each sentence.

showers	building	crops	floods	amount

11. Take your umbrella, because there may be rain _____.

12. Too much rain causes _____.

13. Farmers plant their _____ in fields.

14. There is a new _____ across from my house.

15. A big house has a large _____ of space.

Writing a Description
Draw a picture that shows where you live. Write sentences that tell about your home. Use synonyms to make your sentences interesting.

Antonyms

Have you ever felt cold when a friend felt hot? Then you felt the opposite way your friend did. **Opposite** means "different in every way." The words **cold** and **hot** are **antonyms.** Antonyms are words with opposite meanings.

Read the letter. Look for the antonyms.

Dear Sam,

   You look high and low, but you can't find me! Here are some ideas to help you.

1. Find a bright, sunny spot where I may be asleep.
2. Look up in high places where I like to climb.
3. Look down under the bed. It's dark there.
4. Open a can of food. I'll come running!

Love,

Snowball

Draw lines to match antonyms in the story.

bright	high
low	down
up	dark

Look in the letter for the antonym of the word **close.** Write the word on the line.

_____

Read the story. Look for antonyms.

Lost and Found

Lisa liked to help her teacher. One day Lisa's teacher asked if she would like to help keep the lost and found box neat. "He'll be glad he asked me to help," Lisa thought. The box used to be so messy. Lisa kept it nice and neat.

On her birthday, Lisa spotted a stuffed cat in the box. She loved cats. She picked it up. It was soft and cuddly. Other things in the box were old and dirty. The stuffed cat was clean and new.

Lisa put the cat back in the box. She thought, "Someone will miss this, and she'll come to claim it. I know I would if it was mine."

A week went by. No one claimed the cat. Lisa put the cat in her backpack and took it home. It didn't feel right to play with it, though. It wasn't really hers. "I'll put it back," she said. The next day she took the cat back to school. She sneaked it back into the lost and found box.

That day Lisa's friend Ana looked inside the box. She said, "Someone found your birthday present, Lisa. I lost it on the bus!"

Ana gave the cat to Lisa. "Happy birthday!"

Checking Comprehension

Write the answer to each question on the lines.

1. What kind of person is Lisa? How can you tell?

   _____

   _____

2. Do you think Lisa should have returned the cat to the box? Why or why not?

   _____

   _____

Practicing Comprehension Skills

Write the antonyms for these words in the story.

3. The opposite of **messy** is _____.

4. The opposite of **old** is _____.

5. The opposite of **dirty** is _____.

6. The opposite of **lost** is _____.

Fill in the circle next to the antonym for the underlined word.

7. Lisa thought it was <u>wrong</u> to take the cat.

   ◯ right   ◯ left   ◯ late

8. That <u>day</u> Ana looked in the box.

   ◯ place   ◯ night   ◯ lunch

9. Ana was <u>happy</u> to find the stuffed cat in the box.

⚪ sad ⚪ sleepy ⚪ hungry

Practicing Vocabulary

Write the word from the box that finishes each sentence.

claimed	cuddly	she'll	He'll	present

10. Lisa _____ the prize for being the neatest.

11. Ana needs help, so _____ ask her friend Lisa.

12. _____ look for his watch in the lost and found box.

13. Ana gave Lisa a _____ on her birthday.

14. Lisa's toy cat was soft and _____.

Making the Reading and Writing Connection

Writing an Ad
On another sheet of paper, write sentences to describe something you want to sell. Then use antonyms to change three words in your ad. Have a friend read your funny new ad.

Homonyms

The words **here** and **hear** sound the same, but they are not the same. They mean different things, and they are spelled differently. These words are called **homonyms.** Homonyms are words that **sound** the same, but are **not** the same.

Read the story. Find words that sound the same but have different meanings.

Mom looked in my closet. "Close the door," she told me. My clothes were all too small. We knew we didn't want to sew new clothes. So we went to the store.

We bought eight shirts and a pair of blue pants. Then we saw an ice-cream store. They had pear-flavored ice cream. We ate some. It was better than good. It was great!

Draw lines to match the homonyms.

eight	pear	knew	new
pair	to	close	sew
too	ate	so	clothes

Write a word from the story for each homonym.

blew _____ two _____

Tip

If you don't know which homonym to use in a sentence, look up the words in a dictionary. Use the word that matches your meaning.

Read about Elephant's shopping trip.
Look for homonyms.

The Shopping Trip

Elephant and his mother were shopping at the grocery store. "You can help me look for things," Mama said. "We need apples. Look for a good sale."

Elephant looked and looked. Finally, he saw a sail. He brought the sailboat to Mama. "What is this for?" she asked.

"You said to look for a sail," said Elephant.

Mama laughed and hugged him. "I meant S-A-L-E," she said. "That's a special price on something. Could you look for pears now, Elephant?"

Elephant looked around. He saw oranges, pineapples, and even pears. They were not in pairs, though. Elephant saw a clerk. "Where are the pairs?" he asked.

"What do you need pairs of?" asked the clerk. "Do you need pairs of socks?"

"No," said Elephant. "I think it's something you eat."

"Oh, you mean pears," said the clerk. "Here's a pair of pears." The clerk handed him two pears.

Elephant brought them to his mother. "I have a good idea," he told her. "Next time I will write down what we need. That way, I will be sure to get everything right."

"Good boy!" said Mama. "Now I will pay the clerk what we owe for this fruit. Then we can go home and eat it."

"Yum!" said Elephant.

Checking Comprehension

Write the answer to each question on the lines.

1. Do you think Mama should have written a list for Elephant? Why or why not?

   _____

   _____

2. What do you think Mama and Elephant will do when they get home?

   _____

   _____

Practicing Comprehension Skills

Write the homonym for each of these words in the story.

3. pairs _____   5. oh _____

4. sail _____   6. right _____

Write the word that belongs in each sentence.

7. Elephant went _____ the grocery store.

   two   to   too

8. Mama needed to _____ some fruit.

   by   buy

Write the word that belongs in each sentence.

9. Elephant did not find apples on _____.

                                  sail   sale

10. Elephant found pears _____.

                   their   there   they're

Practicing Vocabulary

Write the word from the box that matches each clue.

finally   everything   grocery   shopping   brought

_____ **11.** all the things

_____ **12.** carried to a place

_____ **13.** at the end

_____ **14.** store that sells food or supplies for the house

_____ **15.** going to buy something

Writing a Shopping List
On another sheet of paper, make a list of six things you would like to buy at a store. Use words that have homonyms, such as **pair, eight,** and **two,** in your shopping list.

Using a Map

A **map** is a drawing that shows how to get from one place to another. Some maps have pictures on them. A **map key** tells you what each picture means. Use the map key and the pictures to figure out where things are on the map.

Look at the map. Then read the story. Use the map to help you understand what you read.

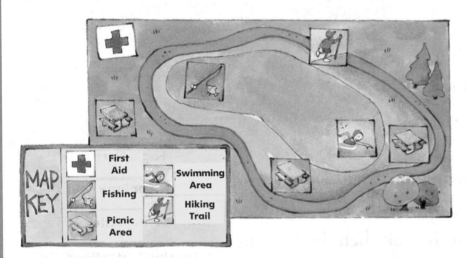

We're going to visit a new park! This park is huge, so we need a map to find all the places.

There are many picnic areas to have lunch. The park has a trail for hiking. There is a big lake with places to fish and swim. What a great way to spend a day!

What can you do in the lake? _____

How many first-aid areas are there? _____

How many picnic areas do you see? _____

Tip

When you read a map, be sure to check the map key. Knowing how to use the map can save you time.

Read the story about a family trip to Animal Land. Use the map to find each place.

A Trip to Animal Land

"Wow! Look at this place!" said Maria and Mark when the family arrived at Animal Land. Many people were on the rides. Families were fishing and riding paddle boats in the pond. Others were having a picnic in the park.

"Let's get a map of Animal Land," said Mom.

The family used the map to find the rides. The first ride was the Eagle Nest. It took them high up in the air. Next, they went on a ride called the Flying Fish and got all wet!

"Let's try the paddle boats!" said Maria. They went to Painted Turtle Pond. While they were there, they saw an eagle fly high overhead.

Afterwards, the family used the map to find Bear Cub Cave. With a guide they explored a real cave!

"We're hungry!" they all said afterward. They took their picnic lunch to Deer Park. What a wonderful place for a family to spend the day!

MAP KEY

Eagle Nest

Deer Park

Flying Fish

Painted Turtle Pond

Bear Cub Cave

Checking Comprehension

Write the answer to each question on the lines.

1. Why did the family need a map of Animal Land?

_____

_____

2. Would you want to visit Animal Land? Why or why not?

_____

Practicing Comprehension Skills

Look at the map. Fill in the circle next to the answer.

3. Following the path, what is closest to Eagle Nest?

○ Bear Cub Cave   ○ Painted Turtle Pond   ○ Flying Fish

4. Which drawing in the map key stands for Deer Park?

○ the eagle   ○ the deer   ○ the turtle

5. Where did the family go after Painted Turtle Pond?

○ Bear Cub Cave   ○ Deer Park   ○ Eagle Nest

6. Read the story again. Then look at the map.
Use a crayon or marker to draw a path on the
map showing each place the family went.

Fill in the circle next to the answer.

7. Where did the family's day at Animal Land end?

○ Deer Park   ○ Bear Cub Cave   ○ Flying Fish

8. What can a family do at Deer Park?

○ fall over   ○ picnic   ○ fish

Practicing Vocabulary

Write a word from the box to finish each sentence.

eagle	explored	paddle	people	wonderful

9. Use a _____ to row a boat.

10. The boy _____ the attic with his parents.

11. Many _____ look at maps to find their way.

12. An _____ makes a nest high up in a tree.

13. It is fun to take trips to _____ places.

Writing Directions
On another sheet of paper, draw a map of your classroom to show where things are. Put a map key on your map. Write three sentences telling how to find something on your map.

Understanding Tables

Sometimes information is easier to understand when it is shown in rows. This is called a **table**. A table is a way of showing information that you want to compare. A table can have words or numbers or both.

Read the story. The table gives more information.

"Great job, Paul!" yelled Ms. Clark, the gym teacher. "Mr. Green's class has another soccer goal."

"How many goals do we have now?" asked Paul.

"Let me check my table. Mr. Green's class has six goals," said Ms. Clark. "I'm keeping track of all the goals scored by each second-grade class."

"Come on! Let's keep playing!" said Paul.

Use the table to write the answers to the questions.

Second Grade Soccer Goals		
Teacher	**Room Number**	**Goals**
Mr. Green	Room 19	6
Mrs. Perez	Room 20	3
Mr. Lee	Room 21	7

Tip

When you read a table, look at the title. Read the headings. Run your finger across each row to help you find the information you want to compare.

How many goals were made by Mrs. Perez's class? _____

What room scored six goals? _____

Which teacher's class scored the most? _____

Read the story. Think about how the table helps you understand what you read.

Let's Play 500!

"I just invented a new game called 500," Jed told his friends. "Every time I throw the ball in the air, I'll shout 50 or 100. If you catch the ball, you score that many points. If you drop the ball, you lose that many points. As soon as someone scores 500 points, it's that person's turn to throw the ball."

Michelle was worried about keeping score. "What if I make a mistake adding up my points?" she asked.

"We'll dislike you for trying to trick us," Miles teased. "Just kidding!" he added. "I'm worried about that, too. I just want to catch the ball. I don't want to worry about adding and subtracting."

"I'm good at math," said Kay. "I'll keep track of everybody's points in my notebook. I'll recount my numbers to make sure the scores are right."

"Thanks, Kay," Tomas told her. "Let's start!"

"Spread out, everybody," Jed shouted. "100!"

Scores for 500		
Name	**Points**	**Totals**
Michelle	100 + 100 + 100 + 100 + 100	500
Miles	100 − 50 + 100 + 100	250
Tomas	100 + 100 + 100	300

Checking Comprehension

Write the answer to each question on the lines.

1. Are you more like Jed or Kay? Tell why.

   _____

   _____

2. How do you get to throw the ball in the game of 500?

Practicing Comprehension Skills

Look at the table Kay made. Then write the answer to each question.

3. What is the name of the table? _____

4. Which children were catching the ball in this

   game of 500? _____

5. Who won this game of 500? _____

6. How many total points did Tomas have? _____

7. Who was throwing the ball in this game? _____

8. Who scored the least points? _____

9. Who will throw the ball next? _____

10. Who caught five balls during this game? _____

Fill in the circle next to the answer.

11. How will the table change when a new game begins?

○ same names   ○ same scores   ○ different names and scores

Practicing Vocabulary

Write the word from the box next to its meaning.

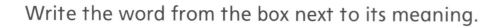

| dislike | everybody | recount | subtracting | worried |

Word	Meaning
12. _____	to add again
13. _____	felt troubled
14. _____	to not like
15. _____	taking away
16. _____	every person

Writing Directions

On another sheet of paper, tell how to play a game you like. Then ask some friends to play your game. Make a table to keep score.

Using Graphs

A **graph** is a picture that shows information. A **circle graph** looks like a pie cut into pieces. A circle graph shows the parts of one whole thing. A big section shows a large amount. A little section shows a small amount.

Read the story. Look at the circle graph.

"What will we see today at the Nature Museum, Mrs. Bailey?" asked Laura.

"There are three special rooms to explore," said Mrs. Bailey. "They show the rain forest, the desert, and the mountains."

"Wow!" shouted Dan. "Let's look at the big waterfall first. It's in the biggest room."

Size of Rooms at the Nature Museum

Rain Forest Room

Mountain Room

Desert Room

Fill in the circle next to the answer.

Which is the smallest room at the Nature Museum?

○ Rain Forest Room   ○ Desert Room   ○ Mountain Room

Write the answer on the line.

Which room is the largest?

_____

Read the story. Think about what the children in the story could show on a circle graph.

Nature Hike

"Be sure to draw all the animals you see. Keep your eyes open. Walk quietly," whispered Mr. Bagly.

Mr. Bagly's class was walking deeper into the woods. Now they were in the thickest part of the forest. People usually did not disturb the animals here. The children hoped to see many types of animals.

"Look!" said Luis softly. "I see a lizard crawling on the ground."

"There are three deer by the lake," Matt said.

"I see four!" Kate whispered.

Mr. Bagly said, "Look up at that nest of robins. How many babies are in the nest?"

"What animal lives down this hole?" asked Chris.

"Look, Chris. Do you see the rabbits?" Mr. Bagly said.

At the end of their hike, the children looked at their pictures. They decided their nature hike was a success!

Checking Comprehension

1. Why did the children whisper and walk quietly?

_____

2. What did the children learn from their hike?

_____

_____

Practicing Comprehension Skills

Look at the circle graph. Write **T** for true and **F** for false next to each question.

Nature Hike Animals

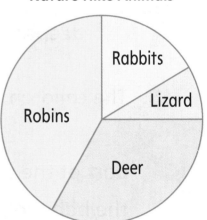

_____ **3.** They saw one lizard.

_____ **4.** They saw squirrels.

_____ **5.** They saw more rabbits than deer.

_____ **6.** They saw more robins than rabbits.

_____ **7.** They saw four kinds of animals.

_____ **8.** They saw the same number of rabbits and lizards.

_____ **9.** They saw more rabbits than lizards.

Write the answer on the line.

10. What animal did they see most?

_____

Look at the circle graph. Fill in the circle next to the answer.

11. Which animal did they see the least?

○ deer   ○ lizard   ○ robins

12. How does the graph show you how much there is of something?

○ the size of each section   ○ the color of each section   ○ the animal names

Practicing Vocabulary

Write the word from the box that belongs in each sentence.

deeper	disturb	forest	success	thickest

13. The children looked for different animals in the

_____. They went into the _____

part of the woods. Their quiet voices did not _____

the baby robins. They hiked _____ into the

woods and saw deer. Seeing so many animals made

their hike a _____.

Making the Reading and Writing Connection

Writing a Description
Write about an animal you have seen. Work together with your classmates to make a circle graph to show which animal was seen the most and which animal was seen the least.

LESSON 30
Using a Dictionary

As you read, you may come to a word that you don't know. You can use a **dictionary** to learn the word's meaning. A dictionary is a book of words and their meanings. The words in a dictionary are in alphabetical order and are called **entry words.** The **guide words** at the top of each page show the first and last entry word on the page.

Read the article about hummingbirds.

Hummingbirds are very unusual birds. Their wings beat around 70 times each second. They can fly up, down, sideways, and backward. They can even hover beside a flower.

Look at the meaning for **hover** in this dictionary. Then answer the question.

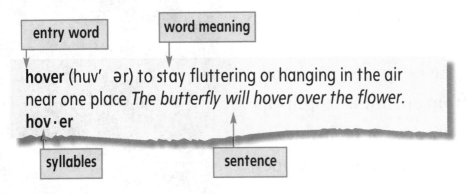

entry word	word meaning

hover (huv' ər) to stay fluttering or hanging in the air near one place *The butterfly will hover over the flower.*
hov·er

syllables	sentence

Tip

If a word has more than one meaning, try reading the sentence with each meaning. Figure out which meaning makes the most sense.

What does the word **hover** mean?

_____

_____

That Sounds Fishy!

Some strange animals live in the sea. These animals act in unusual ways. How many do you know?

An electric eel shocks an animal it wants to eat. A shocked animal can't swim away!

When an enemy comes near, a jawfish spits out small stones to stun its enemy. This gives the jawfish time to escape.

When a cuttlefish sees an enemy, it must act quickly. It squirts out a kind of dark black ink. The inky darkness hides the cuttlefish while it gets away.

A sea cucumber has a long body. Do you know what it does to get away from enemies? It splits its stomach! Then it squirts out some of its insides to surprise its enemy. After the sea cucumber escapes, it regrows the part of its body it squirted.

These are some of the strange and wonderful animals that live in the ocean.

Checking Comprehension

Write the answer to each question on the lines.

1. How do some sea animals protect themselves?

   _____

   _____

2. Which animal do you think is the most unusual?
   Why?

   _____

Practicing Comprehension Skills

Look at these dictionary entries. Then answer the question.

escape > Eskimo

escape (e skāp') 1. to break loose; get free *The bird escaped from its cage.* 2. to keep from getting hurt, killed, or injured *The rabbit escaped the wolf.* **es · cape**

stun > sunny

stun (stun) 1. to make someone unable to feel or think: *A piece of rock stuns the horse.* 2. to shock in a great way *The news of the flood will stun the people.* **stun**

3. What entry words are shown on these dictionary pages?

   _____

Read the sentences. Write **escape** or **stun** in each sentence.

4. A hit on the head can _____ you.

5. The zebra tries to _____ from the lion.

Write your own sentence using each word.

6. escape

_____

7. stun

_____

Practicing Vocabulary

Write the word from the box that belongs in each sentence.

darkness	quickly	stomach	enemy	squirts

8. The _____ makes it hard to see.

9. An animal that wants to eat a fish is its _____.

10. A fast fish swims _____ away from danger.

11. A cuttlefish _____ out a dark black ink.

12. A sea cucumber can grow a new _____.

Writing a Poem
Write a poem about an animal. Find the animal's name in a dictionary. Use the word's meaning for ideas to include in your poem.

Level B Glossary

agree (ə grē´) to have the same opinion

alarms (ə lärmz´) bells, sirens, or other signals that warn of danger or an emergency

amount (ə mount´) quantity

arrived (ə rīvd´) came to a place

artist (ärt´ ist) a person who works in painting, sculpture, music, or any other form of art

asleep (ə slēp´) sleeping

babies (bā´ bēz) very young children

backward (bak´ wərd) toward the back

birthday (bʉrth´ dā) the day on which a person was born

blue (blo͞o) having the color of the clear sky or the deep sea

breakfast (brek´ fəst) the first meal of the day

breathe (brē*th*) to take air into the lungs and then let it out

brought (brôt or brät) carried or led here, or to the place where the speaker would be

building (bil´ diŋ) anything that is built with walls and a roof; for example, a house, factory, or school

careless (ker´ lis) not paying enough attention

cause (kôz or käz) to make happen

city (sit´ ē) a large, important town, usually with many thousands or millions of people

claimed (klāmd) demanded or asked for something that one thinks one has a right to

clapped (klapt) struck the palms of the hand together to show approval

constellations (kän stə lā´ shənz) groups of stars in the sky

cottage (kät´ ij) a small house

country (kun´ trē) land with farms and small towns; land outside of cities

cozy (kō´ zē) warm and comfortable

crops (kräps) farm products that are grown in the soil

crow (krō) to make the shrill cry of a rooster

crumbs (krumz) tiny pieces that are broken off from bread or cake

cuddly (kud´ lē) lovable and cute, or soft and furry, in a way that makes people want to cuddle it

curls (kʉrlz) curves or bends around

darkness (därk´ nəs) the condition of having little or no light

deaf (def) not able to hear

decided (dē sīd´ əd) made up one's mind

decorate (dek´ ər āt) to add something in order to make prettier or more pleasing

deeper (dēp´ ər) farther in or farther back

degrees (də grēz´) units that are used in measuring temperature

desert (dez´ ərt) a dry, sandy region with few or no plants in it

diner (dī´ nər) a small restaurant with a counter

dislike (dis līk´) to have a feeling of not liking

125

disturb (di sturb´) to bother or interrupt

don't (dōnt) do not

dressed (drest) wearing clothes

E

eagle (ē´ gəl) a large, strong bird

easy (ē´ zē) not hard to do, learn, or get; not difficult

elect (ē lekt´) to choose for an office by voting

enemy (en´ ə mē) a person or animal that hates another or fights against another

enjoy (en joi´) to get joy or pleasure from

everybody (ev´ rē bäd´ ē or ev´ rē bud´ ē) every person; everyone

everyone (ev´ rē wun) every person

everything (ev´ rē thiŋ) every thing that there is

exercise (ek´ sər sīz) active use of the body in order to make it stronger or healthier

explored (ek splôrd´) traveled in a region that was not well known, in order to find out more about it

F

far (fär) not near or close

feathers (feth´ ərz) the soft, light parts that grow out of the skin of birds

finally (fī´ nə lē) at the end; at last

floods (fludz) great overflows of water onto a place that is usually dry

food (fōōd) anything that is eaten by an animal or absorbed by a plant to keep up its life and growth

foolish (fōōl´ ish) without good sense; silly

forest (fôr´ əst) a thick growth of trees covering a large piece of land

fresh (fresh) cool and clean

G

getting (get´ iŋ) causing to be

giggling (gig´ liŋ) laughing with high, quick sounds

goal (gōl) the line, net, or any other similar area over or into which a ball or puck must go to score in certain games

good (gōōd) tending to help

government (guv´ ərn mənt) the direction of the affairs of a country, state, or city

great (grāt) fine or excellent

grocery (grō´ sər ē) a store that sells food and household supplies

group (grōōp) a number of related things that form a class

gym (jim) a building or room with equipment for doing exercises and playing games

H

hatch (hach) to bring young animals, such as birds or fish, out of an egg

healthy (hel´ thē) having good health; well

hearty (härt´ ē) warm and friendly

he'll (hēl) he will

helpful (help´ fəl) useful

hold (hōld) to take and keep in the hands or arms

hour (our) any one of the 24 equal parts of a day; 60 minutes

I

important (im pôrt´ nt) having much meaning or value

information (in fər mā´ shən) something that is told or facts that are learned

insects (in´ sekts) tiny animals with six legs, usually two pairs of wings, and a body divided into three parts

inside (in´ sīd´) on or in the part that is within

126

interesting (in´ trist iŋ or in´ tər est iŋ) holding one's interest and attention

J jogger (jäg´ ər) a person who exercises by running at a slow, steady pace

July (jo͞o li´) the seventh month of the year

K knitted (nit´ əd) made by looping yarn or thread together with special needles

L laughed (laft) made some quick sounds with the voice that showed amusement

law (lô or lä) a rule that tells people what they must or must not do

lizard (liz´ ərd) an animal that has a long, slender body and tail, four legs, and scales

M machines (mə shēnz´) things made up of fixed and moving parts, for doing some kind of work

mayor (mā´ ər) the head of the government of a city or town

morning (môrn´ iŋ) the early part of the day, from sunrise to noon

mural (myo͝or´ əl) a large picture or photograph that is painted or put on a wall

museums (myo͞o zē´ əmz) buildings for keeping and showing objects that are important in history, art, or science

N noisy (noi´ zē) making much noise

O odd (äd) not the usual or the regular; strange

office (ôf´ is or äf´ is) the place where a certain kind of business or work is carried on

oven (uv´ ən) a container or enclosed space that is used for baking or roasting food

P paddle (pad´ əl) a short oar that has a wide blade at one or both ends

paintings (pānt´ iŋz) pictures made with paints

patterns (pat´ ərnz) arrangements of parts; designs

people (pē´ pəl) human beings; persons

performers (pər fôrm´ ərz) people who perform for an audience

players (plā´ ərz) people who play a game

playing (plā´ iŋ) having fun

points (points) dots

present (prez´ ənt) a gift

puddle (pud´ əl) a small pool of water

pup (pup) a young dog; puppy

Q quickly (kwik´ lē) in a fast or rapid way

R reason (rē´ zən) the cause for some action or feeling

recount (rē kount´) to count again

returned (rē tʉrnd´) came back

S scientists (sī´ ən tists) experts in science

score (skôr) the number of points made in a contest or game

scrubby (skrub´ ē) small and low to the ground

she'll (shēl) she will

shoelaces (sh ´lās əz) cords, leather, or other materials used for fastening shoes

shook (sho͝ok) moved something quickly up and down or back and forth

shopping (shäp´ iŋ) going to shops to look over and buy things

showers (shou´ ərz) short falls of rain

silly (sil´ ē) not showing or having good sense

sleigh (slā) a carriage with runners instead of wheels that is used to travel over snow or ice

slipped (slipt) slid by accident

smile (smīl) the expression of the face that is made by making the corners of the mouth turn up to show that a person is pleased, happy, or friendly

snake (snāk) a crawling reptile that has a long, thin body and no legs

sorry (sär´ ē) feeling mild regret

space (spās) the distance or area between things

special (spesh´ əl) more than others; main

squirts (skwurts) shoots out in a thin stream; spurts

started (stärt´ əd) began to go, do, or act

starving (stärv´ iŋ) suffering or dying from lack of food

sticky (stik´ ē) holding on to anything that is touched

stomach (stum´ ək) the large, hollow organ into which food goes after it is swallowed

stones (stōnz) small pieces of hard mineral matter that is found in the earth but is not metal

strong (strôŋ) having great power; not weak

subtracting (səb trakt´ iŋ) taking away a part from a whole or one number from another

success (sək ses´) something that turned out well or had the result that was hoped for

surprise (sər prīz´) something that is not expected

T **thank** (thaŋk) to say that one is grateful to another person

thickest (thik´ əst) growing or put most closely together

tied (tīd) equal in points scored

tongue (tuŋ) the movable muscle attached to the bottom of the mouth

treats (trēts) fun things to do or eat

U **until** (un til´) up to the time of

useless (yo͞os´ ləs) having no use; worthless

V **vegetables** (vej´ tə bəlz or vej´ ə tə bəlz) plants, or parts of plants, that are used as food

W **waded** (wād´ əd) walked through something soft or liquid, such as mud or water, that slows a person down

wasn't (wuz´ ənt or wäz´ ənt) was not

watered (wôt´ ərd) put water on or in

whisper (hwis´ pər or wis´ pər) a soft, low way of speaking

wonderful (wun´ dər fəl) very good; excellent

world (wurld) the Earth

worried (wur´ ēd) troubled; anxious